# Introduction

It's time to stop looking and start FINDING what you want on the Internet. With the number of law related sites growing exponentially by the day, you need a resource to help you find the most relevant materials quickly and easily. This guide is that resource. Whether you are a novice or an experienced surfer, this guidebook will show you the most useful legal sites available on the Internet today.

By using the well-defined and logically organized topics you will locate statutes, codes, cases, records, news, people and much, much more. Whenever possible the Internet addresses provided take you through layers of less valuable sites straight to Internet pages rich with relevant and targeted information. As a result of this by-passing of pages you will save the dozens of clicks and hundreds of hours that you would otherwise spend waiting for useless pages to load. Furthermore, these sites, which have been compiled after extensive research, are well established and have proven themselves consistent providers of up-to-date legal materials. The staff at NetGuide has spent innumerable hours looking for only the best, most informative sites and has provided them here in this concise guide.

D1682664

# Contents

This research guide contains information on a variety of topics divided into two general categories-Legal Internet Research and General Internet Research. The resources in the General Internet Research area are invaluable tools which may be used to find information on ANY subject as well as new legal sources as they become available in the future.

## LEGAL INTERNET RESEARCH

### Practice Areas - 13

## GENERAL INTERNET RESEARCH

# How To Use This Book

This guide is your starting point to finding legal information on the Internet. Within its pages you are given the addresses of web sites which are useful in finding information on virtually any legal topic. As you conduct your research over time you will find certain web addresses are used more frequently than others. In order to save time and avoid the unnecessary retyping of web addresses, we encourage you to save your most frequently visited addresses using your Internet browser's "Bookmarking" capabilities. To facilitate this process we have provided brief summaries of the "Bookmarking" functions of both Netscape's Navigator[1] and Microsoft's Internet Explorer[2], the two most common browser programs.

## NETSCAPE NAVIGATOR[1] 4.x

To bookmark a web page:
 1. Go to the web page you want to bookmark.
 2. Click **Bookmarks**. On Mac OS, open the Bookmarks menu--the green bookmark icon to the right of the Go menu.
 3. Choose **Add Bookmark**.
The name of the currently displayed page is added as the last item in the Bookmark menu. To open one of your bookmarked pages, click the **Bookmarks** button and then click the page you want to open.
For more information and instructions on organizing your bookmarks see:

**Help: Help Contents: Index: "Bookmarks"**

## INTERNET EXPLORER[2] 5.x

To add a page to your collection of favorite pages:
 1. Go to the page you want to add to your collection of favorite pages.
 2. On the **Favorites** menu, click **Add to Favorites**.
 3. Type a new name for the page if you want to.
To open one of your favorite pages, click the **Favorites** button on the toolbar, and then click the page you want to open.
For more information and instructions on organizing your favorite pages see:
**Help: Contents and Index: Index: "favorite Web pages"**

[1] Netscape Navigator is a trademark of Netscape Communications Corp. Instructions © 1994-1998 Netscape Communications Corporation. [2] Internet Explorer is a trademark of Microsoft Corp. Instructions © 1999 Microsoft Corp.

# Internet Legal Researching
## MegaLaw Sites
[These are sites which focus almost exclusively on providing a broad range of law related materials ]

| | |
|---|---|
| AllLaw | www.allaw.com |
| American Bar Association Researching | www.abanet.org/lawlink/home.html |
| American Law Sources Online | www.lawsource.com/also |
| Cornell Legal Info. Institute | www.law.cornell.edu |
| Emory Law Library | www.law.emory.edu/LAW/refdesk/toc.html |
| FastSearch Legal Resources | www.fastsearch.com/law/main.htm |
| Findlaw | www.findlaw.com |
| Hieros Gamos | www.hg.org |
| ILRG- [Internet Legal Resource Guide] | www.ilrg.com |
| Internet Law Library | law.house.gov/1.htm |
| Jurist Law Professor's Network | jurist.law.pitt.edu |
| Law.com | www.law.com |
| Law Forum | www.lawforum.net |
| Law Journal Extra! | www.ljx.com |
| Law Library of Congress | lcweb2.loc.gov/glin/lawhome.html |

NOTE: Some browsers require http:// before the listed addresses.

| Law Library Resource Exchange | www.llrx.com |
|---|---|
| LawLinks.com | www.lawlinks.com |
| Law News Network | www.lawnewsnetwork.com |
| Lexis/Nexis | www.lexis.com |
| Piper Resources | www.piperinfo.com/state/states.html |
| Rominger Legal | www.romingerlegal.com |
| The Virtual Chase | www.virtualchase.com |
| Washburn U. School of Law | www.washlaw.edu |
| Westlaw | www.westlaw.com |
| Yahoo Legal Resources | dir.yahoo.com/Government/Law |

## Finding Experts

| Expert Witness Network | www.witness.net |
|---|---|
| Expert Pages | expertpages.com |
| Experts.com | www.experts.com |
| Findlaw Experts | www.findlaw.com/13experts/witness.html |
| Hieros Gamos: Experts | www.hg.org/expert-serv.html |
| National Dir. Of Expert Witnesses | www.claims.com/online.html |

NOTE: Some browsers require http:// before the listed addresses.

# Contents

This research guide contains information on a variety of topics divided into two general categories-Legal Internet Research and General Internet Research. The resources in the General Internet Research area are invaluable tools which may be used to find information on ANY subject as well as new legal sources as they become available in the future.

## LEGAL INTERNET RESEARCH

### Practice Areas - 13

## GENERAL INTERNET RESEARCH

# Internet Legal Researching

## MegaLaw Sites

[These are sites which focus almost exclusively on providing a broad range of law related materials ]

| | |
|---|---|
| AllLaw | www.allaw.com |
| American Bar Association Researching | www.abanet.org/lawlink/home.html |
| American Law Sources Online | www.lawsource.com/also |
| Cornell Legal Info. Institute | www.law.cornell.edu |
| Emory Law Library | www.law.emory.edu/LAW/refdesk/toc.html |
| FastSearch Legal Resources | www.fastsearch.com/law/main.htm |
| Findlaw | www.findlaw.com |
| Hieros Gamos | www.hg.org |
| ILRG- [Internet Legal Resource Guide] | www.ilrg.com |
| Internet Law Library | law.house.gov/1.htm |
| Jurist Law Professor's Network | jurist.law.pitt.edu |
| Law.com | www.law.com |
| Law Forum | www.lawforum.net |
| Law Journal Extra! | www.ljx.com |
| Law Library of Congress | lcweb2.loc.gov/glin/lawhome.html |

NOTE:  Some browsers require http:// before the listed addresses.

## Finding Firms/Attorneys

| Findlaw | www.findlaw.com/14firms/directories.html |
|---|---|
| Martindale Hubbel | www.martindale.com/locator |
| West's Legal Directory | www.wld.com |

## Fee Based Legal Tools

| BNA [Bureau of National Affairs, Inc.] | www.bna.com | BNA is a leading publisher of print and electronic news and information on developments in law, health care, business, economics,  and other public policy and regulatory areas. |
|---|---|---|
| CourtLink | www.courtlink.com | Combine federal and state search results on one report and obtain case summaries, names, dockets, judgments, claims, creditors and charges. |
| Current Legal | www.currentlegal.com | A full suite of primary legal materials including custom products which allow customers to determine what combination of laws, rules and regulations they need. |
| LOIS  [Law Office Information Systems, Inc.] | www.pita.com | Its state libraries contain case law, statutes, administrative codes, court rules, jury instructions, attorney general opinions, and more. |
| Oliver's Cases | www.oliverscases.com | Customized online delivery of federal and state appellate court opinions. |
| Versus | www.versuslaw.com | Searchable state & federal appellate decisions |

NOTE:  Some browsers require http:// before the listed addresses.

| | |
|---|---|
| LJX! Arbitration & ADR | www.ljextra.com/practice/arbitration/index.html |
| Mediation Information and Resource Center | www.mediate.com/resolution.cfm |

**ANTITRUST**

| | |
|---|---|
| ABA Antitrust Division | www.abanet.org/antitrust/home.html |
| Antitrust Policy Page | www.antitrust.org |
| Antitrust Case Summary Browser | $w^3$.stolaf.edu/people/becker/antitrust/antitrust.html |
| Antitrust Law & Economics Review | webpages.metrolink.net/~cmueller |
| DOJ Antitrust Division | www.usdoj.gov/atr/index.html |
| FindLaw Antitrust Law | www.findlaw.com/01topics/01antitrust/index.html |
| Internet Law Library Antitrust Materials | law.house.gov/315.htm |
| LII Antitrust Law Materials | www.law.cornell.edu/topics/antitrust.html |
| LJX! Antitrust Law | www.ljextra.com/practice/antitrust/index.html |
| Web Counsel Antitrust Resources | www.webcounsel.com/antitrus.htm |

**BANKRUPTCY**

| | |
|---|---|
| American Bankruptcy Institute | www.abiworld.org |
| Bankruptcy Online | www.fedfil.com/bankruptcy |

NOTE:  Some browsers require http:// before the listed addresses  -  $w^3$ = www.

| Telecom Info. Resources on the Internet | china.si.umich.edu/telecom/telecom-info.html |
|---|---|
| **CONSTITUTIONAL** | |
| FindLaw: Constitutional Law Materials | w³.findlaw.com/01topics/06onstitutional/index.html |
| Hieros Gamos Constitutional Law | www.hg.org/conlaw.html |
| International Constitutional Law Index | www.uni-wuerzburg.de/law/index.html |
| LII Constitutional Law Materials | www.law.cornell.edu/topics/constitutional.html |
| LJX! Constitutional Law | www.ljextra.com/practice/constitutional/index.html |
| WWW Virtual Law Library Constitutional Law | www.law.indiana.edu/law/v-lib/constit.html |
| U.S. Constitution - Analysis & Interpretation | w³.access.gpo.gov/congress/senate/constitution/toc.html |
| **CONTRACTS** | |
| FindLaw Contract Law | www.findlaw.com/01topics/07contracts/index.html |
| Hieros Gamos Contract Law | www.hg.org/commerc.html |
| LII Contracts Law Materials | www.law.cornell.edu/topics/contracts.html |
| The Center for Research on Contracts | crcse.business.pitt.edu |
| Uniform Commercial Code | www.law.cornell.edu/ucc/ucc.table.html |
| WWW Virtual Law Library Contracts Law | www.law.indiana.edu/law/v-lib/contracts.html |

NOTE:  Some browsers require http:// before the listed addresses  -  w³ = www.

## Travel Related Sites

| | |
|---|---|
| Airline Phone Numbers & Web Sites | www.princeton.edu/Main/air800.html |
| Association of Business Travelers | www.abt-travel.com |
| Flifo Travel Agent | www.flifo.com |
| The Internet Travel Network | www.itn.net |
| TheTrip.com | www.thetrip.com |
| Travelocity Travel Agent | www.travelocity.com |
| Travelweb Agent | www.travelweb.com |

## News and Information

| | |
|---|---|
| ABC News | abcnews.go.com |
| Associated Press News Wire | wire.ap.org |
| C-SPAN | www.c-span.org |
| CBS News | www.cbs.com/navbar/news.html |
| CNN | www.cnn.com |
| LATimes | www.latimes.com |
| NBC News | nbc.com |
| News Edge Newspage | www.newspage.com |
| NY Times | www.nytimes.com |

NOTE: Some browsers require http:// before the listed addresses.

# General Tips/Techniques

★ When searching for a company or entity try to use www.entityname.com
e.g. www.ford.com.

★ When a page does not load try to move "up" a level by deleting everything to the right of the
last "/" symbol in the URL address window. Keep trying this until the page will load.
e.g. www.legal.com/home/pages.htm will not load therefore try www.legal.com/home/ if this does not
load try www.legal.com/.

★ Use your browser's "find in page" or "find in frame" commands to locate words within text
intensive sites. In Nestscape Navigator 4.x & Internet Explorer 5.x go to Edit then select "Find in
Page".

★ Use your browser's "Open in New Window" command to utilize several browser windows at once. This
will GREATLY increase your researching speed. To use this feature simply place the cursor over the site
you would like to visit then click on the right mouse button and select "Open in New Window". Using this
command will NOT close the window from which you selected the next site but will minimize it instead. To
move between open/minimized windows click on the rectangular boxes located on the taskbar which lies
at the bottom of your screen.

## Finding Firms/Attorneys

| Findlaw | www.findlaw.com/14firms/directories.html |
|---------|-------------------------------------------|
| Martindale Hubbel | www.martindale.com/locator |
| West's Legal Directory | www.wld.com |

## Fee Based Legal Tools

| BNA [Bureau of National Affairs, Inc.] | www.bna.com | BNA is a leading publisher of print and electronic news and information on developments in law, health care, business, economics, and other public policy and regulatory areas. |
|---|---|---|
| CourtLink | www.courtlink.com | Combine federal and state search results on one report and obtain case summaries, names, dockets, judgments, claims, creditors and charges. |
| Current Legal | www.currentlegal.com | A full suite of primary legal materials including custom products which allow customers to determine what combination of laws, rules and regulations they need. |
| LOIS [Law Office Information Systems, Inc.] | www.pita.com | Its state libraries contain case law, statutes, administrative codes, court rules, jury instructions, attorney general opinions, and more. |
| Oliver's Cases | www.oliverscases.com | Customized online delivery of federal and state appellate court opinions. |
| Versus | www.versuslaw.com | Searchable state & federal appellate decisions |

NOTE: Some browsers require http:// before the listed addresses.

# Writing Aids

| DICTIONARIES/ENCYCLOPEDIAS | |
|---|---|
| Duhaim's Law Dictionary | wwlia.org:80/diction.htm |
| Nolo's Legal Encyclopedia | www.nolo.com/briefs.html |
| OneLook Dictionary | www.onelook.com |
| Shark Talk Dictionary | www.nolo.com/dictionary/wordindex.cfm |
| Wordsmyth Dictionary & Thesaurus | www.lightlink.com/bobp/wedt |
| West's Legal Topics | www1.wld.com/ldweal.htm |
| West's Legal Dictionary | www1.wld.com/ldorans.htm |
| OTHER AIDS | |
| Blue Book | www.law.cornell.edu/citation/citation.table.html |
| Columbia Guide to Online Citation | www.columbia.edu/cu/cup/cgos |
| Familiar Quotations | www.columbia.edu/acis/bartleby/bartlett |
| Online English Grammar | www.edunet.com/english/grammar/index.html |
| Roget's Thesaurus | humanities.uchicago.edu/forms_unrest/ROGET.html |
| Shepard's | www.bender.com |
| Strunk: Elements of Style | www.columbia.edu/acis/bartleby/strunk |

NOTE: Some browsers require http:// before the listed addresses.

# Federal Law Resources

## Law/Rules

**Code of Federal Regulations (CFR)**
www.gpo.ucop.edu/search/cfr.html

**Federal Register (FR)**
www.gpo.ucop.edu/search/default.html

**Rules of Appellate Procedure**
www.dcd.uscourts.gov/frap-index.html

**Rules of Civil Procedure**
www.law.cornell.edu/rules/frcp

**Rules of Criminal Procedure**
www.dcd.uscourts.gov/frcrp-index.html

**Rules of Evidence**
www.law.cornell.edu/rules/fre

**U.S. Constitution**
www.law.cornell.edu:80/constitution/constitution.overview.html

**U.S. Code**
www.gpo.ucop.edu:80/search/uscode.html **OR**
www.law.cornell.edu/uscode

## Federal Information Gateways

**All Law - Federal Information**
www.alllaw.com/law/federal_law

**American Law Source Online - Fed. Gov.**
www.lawsource.com/also/usa.cgi?us1

**Emory Law Library - U.S. Government**
www.law.emory.edu/LAW/refdesk/country/us/fedag.html

**Fed. Gov. Info. Exchange - A-Z Directory**
www.info.gov/fed_directory/list_a-d.shtml

**Federal Web Locator**
www.law.vill.edu/fed-agency/fedwebloc.html

**FedLaw**
www.legal.gsa.gov

**FedWorld.gov**
www.fedworld.gov

**Government Printing Office**
www.gpo.gov

NOTE: Some browsers require http:// before the listed addresses.

**Library of Congress Internet Resource Page**
lcweb.loc.gov/global/state/stategov.html

**LSU Library - U.S. Fed. Gov. Agencies Dir.**
www.lib.lsu.edu/gov/fedgov.html

**WWW Virtual Library: Law : U.S. Gov.**
www.law.indiana.edu/law/v-lib/us-gov.html

## Federal Government Sites

**Department of Commerce**
www.doc.gov

**Department of Energy**
www.doe.gov

**Department of Health and Human Services**
www.os.dhhs.gov

**Department of Justice (DOJ)**
www.usdoj.gov

**Department of Labor**
www.dol.gov

**Department of Transportation (DOT)**
www.dot.gov

**Environmental Protection Agency (EPA)**
www.epa.gov

**Federal Communications Commission (FCC)**
www.fcc.gov

**Internal Revenue Service (IRS)**
www.irs.gov

**Library of Congress**
lcWeb.loc.gov/homepage/lchp.html

**National Archives & Records Administration**
www.nara.gov

**National Labor Relations Board (NLRB)**
www.nlrb.gov

**Securities and Exchange Commission (SEC)**
www.sec.gov

**U.S. Copyright Office**
lcweb.loc.gov/copyright

**U.S. Patent and Trademark Office**
www.uspto.gov

**U.S. Census Bureau**
www.census.gov

NOTE: Some browsers require http:// before the listed addresses.

## Courts with Opinions

| | |
|---|---|
| Index | www.ll.georgetown.edu/Fed-Ct   OR   www.findlaw.com/casecode/courts |
| SCt. | supct.law.cornell.edu/supct   OR   www.ll.georgetown.edu:80/Fed-Ct/supreme.html |
| 1st Cir. | www.law.emory.edu/1circuit |
| 2nd Cir. | www.law.pace.edu/lawlib/legal/us-legal/judiciary/second-circuit.html |
| 3rd Cir. | www.law.vill.edu/Fed-Ct/ca03.html |
| 4th Cir. | www.law.emory.edu/4circuit |
| 5th Cir. | www.law.utexas.edu/us5th |
| 6th Cir. | www.law.emory.edu/6circuit |
| 7th Cir. | www.kentlaw.edu/7circuit |
| 8th Cir. | ls.wustl.edu/8th.cir |
| 9th Cir. | www.law.vill.edu/Fed-Ct/ca09.html |
| 10th Cir. | lawlib.wuacc.edu/ca10 |
| 11th Cir. | www.law.emory.edu/11circuit |
| D.C. Cir. | www.ll.georgetown.edu:80/Fed-Ct/cadc.html |
| Fed. Cir. | www.ll.georgetown.edu/Fed-Ct/cafed.html |

NOTE:  Some browsers require http:// before the listed addresses.

# State Law Resources
## MegaLaw Sites- State Indices

| | |
|---|---|
| American Law Sources Online | www.lawsource.com/also |
| FindLaw | www.findlaw.com/11stategov/index.html |
| Hieros Gamos | www.hg.org/usstates.html |
| Internet Law Library | law.house.gov/17.htm |
| Internet Legal Resource Guide | www.ilrg.com/gov.html |
| Law Journal Extra! | lawonline.ljx.com/courts/states/index.html |
| Law.com | www.law.com |
| Legal Forms | www.uslegalforms.com/free.htm |
| Legal Online | www.legalonline.com/statute2.htm |
| Legal Information Institute | www.law.cornell.edu/states/listing.html |
| Municipal Code Corporation | www.municode.com/database.html |
| Municipal Codes Online | www.spl.org/govpubs/municode.html |
| National Center for State Courts | www.ncsc.dni.us/court/sites/courts.htm |
| Piper Resources | www.piperinfo.com/state/states.html |
| Rominger Legal | www.romingerlegal.com/states.htm |
| Washburn U. School of Law | lawlib.wuacc.edu/washlaw/uslaw/statelaw.html |

NOTE: Some browsers require http:// before the listed addresses.

| | State Home Page | Legislative Home | Judicial Home |
|---|---|---|---|
| AK | www.state.ak.us | www.legis.state.ak.us | www.alaska.net/~akctlib/homepage.htm |
| AL | www.state.al.us | www.legislature.state.al.us | www.alalinc.net/system.htm |
| AR | www.state.ar.us | www.arkleg.state.ar.us | courts.state.ar.us |
| AZ | www.state.az.us | www.azleg.state.az.us | www.supreme.state.az.us/welcome.htm |
| CA | www.state.ca.us | www.assembly.ca.gov | www.courtinfo.ca.gov |
| CO | www.state.co.us | w$^3$.state.co.us/gov_dir/stateleg.html | www.courts.state.co.us/ct-index.htm |
| CT | www.state.ct.us | www.cga.state.ct.us | www.jud.state.ct.us |
| DE | www.state.de.us | w$^3$.state.de.us/research/assembly.htm | www.lawlib.widener.edu/pages/deopind.htm |
| FL | www.state.fl.us | www.leg.state.fl.us | www.flcourts.org |
| GA | www.state.ga.us | www2.state.ga.us/legis | www.doas.state.ga.us/courts/supreme |
| HI | www.state.hi.us | telnet://fyi.uhcc.hawaii.edu | www.hawaii.gov/jud/index.html |
| IA | www.state.ia.us | www.legis.state.ia.us | www.judicial.state.ia.us |
| ID | www.state.id.us | w$^3$.state.id.us/legislat/legislat.html | www2.state.id.us/judicial/judicial.html |
| IL | www.state.il.us | www.legis.state.il.us | www.state.il.us/court |
| IN | www.state.in.us | www.state.in.us/legislative | www.state.in.us/judiciary |
| KS | www.state.ks.us | www.state.ks.us/public/legislative | w$^3$.law.ukans.edu/kscourts/kscourts.html |

NOTE: Some browsers require http:// before the listed addresses - w$^3$ = www.

| KY | www.state.ky.us | www.lrc.state.ky.us/home.htm | www.aoc.state.ky.us/intro.htm |
|----|-----------------|-------------------------------|--------------------------------|
| LA | www.state.la.us | www.legis.state.la.us | www.state.la.us/state/judicial.htm |
| MA | www.state.ma.us | www.state.ma.us/legis/legis.htm | www.state.ma.us/courts/courts.htm |
| MD | www.state.md.us | mlis.state.md.us | www.courts.state.md.us |
| ME | www.state.me.us | $w^3$.state.me.us/legis/homepage.htm | www.courts.state.me.us |
| MI | www.state.mi.us | www.michiganlegislature.org | www.migov.state.mi.us/judicial.html |
| MN | www.state.mn.us | www.leg.state.mn.us | www.courts.state.mn.us/index.html |
| MO | www.state.mo.us | www.moga.state.mo.us | www.osca.state.mo.us |
| MS | www.state.ms.us | www.ls.state.ms.us | www.mssc.state.ms.us/default.asp |
| MT | www.state.mt.us | $w^3$.state.mt.us/leg/branch/branch.htm | www.lawlibrary.mt.gov/opinins.htm |
| NC | www.state.nc.us | www.ncga.state.nc.us/index.shtml | www.aoc.state.nc.us |
| ND | www.state.nd.us | www.state.nd.us/lr | www.court.state.nd.us |
| NE | www.state.ne.us | $w^3$.unicam.state.ne.us/index.htm | www.state.ne.us/court/index.html |
| NH | www.state.nh.us | $w^3$.state.nh.us/gencourt/gencourt.htm | www.state.nh.us/courts/home.htm |
| NJ | www.state.nj.us | www.njleg.state.nj.us | www.state.nj.us/judiciary |
| NM | www.state.nm.us | legis.state.nm.us | www.nmcourts.com/disclaim.htm |
| NV | www.state.nv.us | www.leg.state.nv.us/index.htm | www.clan.lib.nv.us/docs/NSCL/nscl.htm |

NOTE:  Some browsers require http:// before the listed addresses  -  $w^3$ = www.

10

| NY | www.state.ny.us | gopher://leginfo.lbdc.state.ny.us | ucs.ljx.com |
|---|---|---|---|
| OH | www.state.oh.us | www.ohio.gov/ohio/legislat.htm | www.sconet.ohio.gov/navigat.htm |
| OK | www.state.ok.us | www.lsb.state.ok.us | www.oscn.net |
| OR | www.state.or.us | www.leg.state.or.us | 159.121.112.45 |
| PA | www.state.pa.us | www.legis.state.pa.us | www.courts.state.pa.us |
| RI | www.state.ri.us | w³.state.ri.us/submenus/leglink.htm | www.ribar.com/Courts/courts.html |
| SC | www.state.sc.us | w³.lpitr.state.sc.us/homepage.htm | www.state.sc.us/judicial |
| SD | www.state.sd.us | w³.state.sd.us/state/legis/lrc.htm | www.state.sd.us/state/judicial |
| TN | www.state.tn.us | www.legislature.state.tn.us | tscaoc.tsc.state.tn.us |
| TX | www.state.tx.us | www.capitol.state.tx.us | www.courts.state.tx.us |
| UT | www.state.ut.us | www.le.state.ut.us | courtlink.utcourts.gov/opinions |
| VA | www.state.va.us | legis.state.va.us/vaonline/v.htm | www.courts.state.va.us/main.htm |
| VT | www.state.vt.us | www.leg.state.vt.us | www.state.vt.us/courts |
| WA | www.state.wa.us | w³.leg.wa.gov/wsladm/default.htm | 198.187.0.226/courts/home.htm |
| WI | www.state.wi.us | www.legis.state.wi.us | www.courts.state.wi.us |
| WV | www.state.wv.us | www.legis.state.wv.us/legishp.html | www.state.wv.us/wvsca |
| WY | www.state.wy.us | legisweb.state.wy.us | courts.state.wy.us |

NOTE: Some browsers require http:// before the listed addresses - w³ = www.

# State Bars

| | | | | | |
|---|---|---|---|---|---|
| **AK** | www.alaskabar.org | **KY** | www.kybar.org | **NY** | www.nysba.org |
| **AL** | www.alabar.org | **LA** | www.lsba.org | **OH** | www.ohiobar.org |
| **AR** | www.arkbar.com | **MA** | www.massbar.org | **OK** | www.okbar.org |
| **AZ** | www.azbar.org | **MD** | www.msba.org | **OR** | www.osbar.org |
| **CA** | www.calbar.org | **ME** | www.mainebar.org | **PA** | www.pabar.org |
| **CO** | www.cobar.org | **MI** | www.michbar.org | **RI** | ribar.com |
| **CT** | www.ctbar.org | **MN** | www.mnbar.org | **SC** | www.scbar.org |
| **DC** | www.dcbar.org | **MO** | www.mobar.org | **SD** | www.sdbar.org |
| **DE** | www.dsba.org | **MS** | www.msbar.org | **TN** | www.tba.org |
| **FL** | www.flabar.org | **MT** | www.montanabar.org | **TX** | www.texasbar.com |
| **GA** | www.gabar.org | **NC** | www.ncbar.org | **UT** | www.utahbar.org |
| **HI** | www.hsba.org | **ND** | N/A | **VA** | www.vsb.org |
| **IA** | www.iowabar.org | **NM** | www.nmbar.org | **WV** | www.wvbar.org |
| **ID** | www.state.id.us/isb | **NE** | www.nebar.com | **VT** | www.vtbar.org |
| **IL** | www.illinoisbar.org | **NH** | www.nh.com/legal/nhbar | **WA** | www.wsba.org |
| **IN** | www.ai.org/isba | **NJ** | www.njsba.com | **WI** | www.wisbar.org |
| **KS** | www.ksbar.org | **NV** | www.nvbar.org | **WY** | www.wyomingbar.org |

NOTE: Some browsers require http:// before the listed addresses.

# Law by Practice Area

## MegaLaw Sites- Area Indices

| | |
|---|---|
| American Law Sources Online | www.lawsource.com/also/usa.cgi?us3#X3Q |
| American Bar Association | www.abanet.org/sections.html |
| FindLaw | www.findlaw.com/01topics/index.html |
| Hieros Gamos | www.hg.org/hg2.html |
| Internet Law Library | law.house.gov/90.htm |
| Internet Legal Resource Guide | www.ilrg.com/subject_ref.html |
| Law News Network | www.lawnewsnetwork.com |
| Legal Information Institute | www.law.cornell.edu/topics/topic1.html (Alphabetical) |
| | www.law.cornell.edu/topics/topic2.html (Categorized) |
| Washburn U. School of Law | www.washlaw.edu/subject/subject.html |
| WWW Virtual Law Library | www.law.indiana.edu/law/v-lib/#topic |

★    If you can not find an area listed in the following table try the more extensive lists which are available at the MegaLaw Area Indices provided above.

★    Use the following area specific sites as a resource to find other sites available in your area.

# Area Specific Materials

| ADMINISTRATIVE LAW | |
| --- | --- |
| ABA Administrative and Regulatory Law Section | www.abanet.org/adminlaw/home.html |
| ABA Administrative Procedure Database | www.law.fsu.edu/library/admin |
| FindLaw Administrative Law | w$^3$.findlaw.com/01topics/00administrative/index.html |
| Heiros Gamos - Administrative Law | www.hg.org/adm.html |
| LII Administrative Law Materials | www.law.cornell.edu/topics/administrative.html |
| LJX! Administrative Law News | w$^3$.ljextra.com/practice/administrative/index.html |
| Nat. Assoc. of Sec. of State - Admin. Rules | www.nass.org/acr/acrdir.htm |
| WWW Virtual Law Library Administrative Law | www.law.indiana.edu/law/v-lib/admin.html |
| ALTERNATIVE DISPUTE RESOLUTION | |
| American Arbitration Association | www.adr.org |
| FindLaw Dispute Resolution and Arbitration | w$^3$.findlaw.com/01topics/11disputeres/index.html |
| Hieros Gamos Alternative Dispute Resolution | www.hg.org/adr.html |
| Internet Law Library ADR | law.house.gov/314.htm |
| LII Alternative Dispute Resolution | www.law.cornell.edu/topics/adr.html |

NOTE: Some browsers require http:// before the listed addresses - w$^3$ = www.

| | |
|---|---|
| LJX! Arbitration & ADR | www.ljextra.com/practice/arbitration/index.html |
| Mediation Information and Resource Center | www.mediate.com/resolution.cfm |

**ANTITRUST**

| | |
|---|---|
| ABA Antitrust Division | www.abanet.org/antitrust/home.html |
| Antitrust Policy Page | www.antitrust.org |
| Antitrust Case Summary Browser | $w^3$.stolaf.edu/people/becker/antitrust/antitrust.html |
| Antitrust Law & Economics Review | webpages.metrolink.net/~cmueller |
| DOJ Antitrust Division | www.usdoj.gov/atr/index.html |
| FindLaw Antitrust Law | www.findlaw.com/01topics/01antitrust/index.html |
| Internet Law Library Antitrust Materials | law.house.gov/315.htm |
| LII Antitrust Law Materials | www.law.cornell.edu/topics/antitrust.html |
| LJX! Antitrust Law | www.ljextra.com/practice/antitrust/index.html |
| Web Counsel Antitrust Resources | www.webcounsel.com/antitrus.htm |

**BANKRUPTCY**

| | |
|---|---|
| American Bankruptcy Institute | www.abiworld.org |
| Bankruptcy Online | www.fedfil.com/bankruptcy |

NOTE:  Some browsers require http:// before the listed addresses  -  $w^3$ = www.

| | |
|---|---|
| FindLaw Bankruptcy Law | w³.findlaw.com/01topics/03bankruptcy/index.html |
| Hieros Gamos Bankruptcy Law | www.hg.org/bankrpt.html |
| Internet Bankruptcy Library | bankrupt.com |
| Internet Law Library Bankruptcy Materials | law.house.gov/311.htm |
| LII Bankruptcy Law Materials | www.law.cornell.edu/topics/bankruptcy.html |
| LJX! Bankruptcy Law | www.ljextra.com/practice/bankruptcy/index.html |
| The Bankruptcy Lawfinder | www.agin.com/lawfind |
| **COMMUNICATIONS** | |
| ACA Center for Communication Law | www.americancomm.org/~aca/american.htm |
| Federal Communications Law Journal | www.law.indiana.edu/fclj/pubs/pubs.html |
| Federal Communications Commission | www.fcc.gov |
| FindLaw Communications Law | w³.findlaw.com/01topics/05communications/index.html |
| Hieros Gamos Communications Law | www.hg.org/communi.html |
| Internet Law Library Communications Materials | law.house.gov/94.htm |
| LII Communications Law Materials | www.law.cornell.edu/topics/communications.html |
| LJX! Communications Law | w³.ljextra.com/practice/communications/index.html |

NOTE: Some browsers require http:// before the listed addresses - w³ = www.

| Telecom Info. Resources on the Internet | china.si.umich.edu/telecom/telecom-info.html |
|---|---|
| **CONSTITUTIONAL** | |
| FindLaw: Constitutional Law Materials | w$^3$.findlaw.com/01topics/06onstitutional/index.html |
| Hieros Gamos Constitutional Law | www.hg.org/conlaw.html |
| International Constitutional Law Index | www.uni-wuerzburg.de/law/index.html |
| LII Constitutional Law Materials | www.law.cornell.edu/topics/constitutional.html |
| LJX! Constitutional Law | www.ljextra.com/practice/constitutional/index.html |
| WWW Virtual Law Library Constitutional Law | www.law.indiana.edu/law/v-lib/constit.html |
| U.S. Constitution - Analysis & Interpretation | w$^3$.access.gpo.gov/congress/senate/constitution/toc.html |
| **CONTRACTS** | |
| FindLaw Contract Law | www.findlaw.com/01topics/07contracts/index.html |
| Hieros Gamos Contract Law | www.hg.org/commerc.html |
| LII Contracts Law Materials | www.law.cornell.edu/topics/contracts.html |
| The Center for Research on Contracts | crcse.business.pitt.edu |
| Uniform Commercial Code | www.law.cornell.edu/ucc/ucc.table.html |
| WWW Virtual Law Library Contracts Law | www.law.indiana.edu/law/v-lib/contracts.html |

NOTE: Some browsers require http:// before the listed addresses - w$^3$ = www.

| CORPORATE/BUSINESS | |
|---|---|
| Company Sleuth | www.companysleuth.com |
| FindLaw Corporate Law | www.findlaw.com/01topics/08corp/index.html |
| Hieros Gamos Corporate Law | www.hg.org/corp.html |
| Internet Law Library Corporations Materials | law.house.gov/329.htm |
| LII Corporations Materials | www.law.cornell.edu/topics/corporations.html |
| LJX! Corporations Law | www.ljextra.com/practice/corporate/index.html |
| SEC | www.sec.gov |
| SEC Edgar Database | www.sec.gov/edgarhp.htm |
| SECLaw.Com | www.seclaw.com |
| CRIMINAL | |
| ACLU Criminal Justice Index | www.aclu.org/issues/criminal/ircj.html |
| CopNet | police.sas.ab.ca |
| FindLaw Criminal Law | www.findlaw.com/01topics/09criminal/index.html |
| Hieros Gamos Criminal Law | www.hg.org/crime.html |
| Internet Law Library Criminal Materials | law.house.gov/96.htm |

NOTE: Some browsers require http:// before the listed addresses - w³ = www.

| Justice Information Center | ncjrs.aspensys.com |
|---|---|
| LII Criminal Law Materials | www.law.cornell.edu/topics/criminal.html |
| LJX! Criminal Law | www.ljextra.com/practice/criminal/index.html |
| National Archive of Criminal Justice Data | www.icpsr.umich.edu/NACJD/home.html |
| WWW Virtual Law Library Criminal Law | www.law.indiana.edu/law/v-lib/criminal.html |
| **ENVIRONMENTAL** | |
| ABA Natural Resources, Environment, Energy Sec. | www.abanet.org/sonreel/home.html |
| Earthlaw | www.earthlaw.org |
| ECONet | www.igc.org/igc/econet |
| Environmental Law Alliance Worldwide | www.igc.apc.org/elaw |
| EPA | www.epa.gov |
| FindLaw Environmental Law | w³.findlaw.com/01topics/13environmental/index.html |
| Hieros Gamos Environmental Law | www.hg.org/environ.html |
| Internet Law Library Environmental Materials | law.house.gov/101.htm |
| LII Environmental Law Materials | www.law.cornell.edu/topics/environmental.html |
| LJX! Environmental Law | www.ljextra.com/practice/environment/index.html |

NOTE: Some browsers require http:// before the listed addresses - w³ = www.

| | |
|---|---|
| WWW Virtual Law Library Environmental Law | www.law.indiana.edu/law/v-lib/envlaw.html |
| **FAMILY** | |
| ABA Commission on Domestic Violence | www.abanet.org/domviol/home.html |
| ABA Family Law Section | www.abanet.org/family/home.html |
| Adoption Statutes, Legislative Code and Links | www.plumsite.com/shea/states.html |
| DivorceNet | www.law.cornell.edu/topics/topic2.html |
| DivorceSource | www.divorcesource.com |
| FindLaw Family Law | www.findlaw.com/01topics/15family/index.html |
| Hieros Gamos Family Law | www.hg.org/family.html |
| Internet Law Library Domestic Relations Materials | law.house.gov/97.htm |
| LII Family Law Materials | www.law.cornell.edu/topics/topic2.html#familylaw |
| LJX! Family Law | www.ljextra.com/practice/family/index.html |
| WWW Virtual Law Library Family Law | www.law.indiana.edu/law/v-lib/family.html |
| **GOVERNMENT CONTRACTS** | |
| Federal Acquisition Jumpstation | nais.nasa.gov/fedproc/home.html |
| FindLaw Government Contracts | w³.findlaw.com/01topics/18govcontracts/index.html |

NOTE: Some browsers require http:// before the listed addresses - w³ = www.

| GovCon | www.govcon.com/ |
|---|---|
| Hieros Gamos Government Law | www.hg.org/govern.html |
| LII Government Contracts Materials | $w^3$.law.cornell.edu/topics/government_contracts.html |
| The Federal Marketplace | www.fedmarket.com |
| U.S. Government Printing Office | www.access.gpo.gov/su_docs |
| **HEALTH** | |
| FastSearch Medical Resources | www.fastsearch.com/med/index.html |
| LII Health Law Materials | www.law.cornell.edu/topics/health.html |
| LJX! Health Law | www.ljextra.com/practice/health/index.html |
| Hieros Gamos Health Law | www.hg.org/health.html |
| FindLaw Health Law | www.findlaw.com/01topics/19health/index.html |
| Internet Law Library Health Law | law.house.gov/103.htm |
| Center for Health Law Studies | lawlib.slu.edu/healthcenter/research/research_index.htm |
| **IMMIGRATION** | |
| American Immigration Resources on the Internet | www.immigration-usa.com/resource.html |
| Department of Labor Immigration Collection | www.oalj.dol.gov/libina.htm |

NOTE: Some browsers require http:// before the listed addresses - $w^3$ = www.

| | |
|---|---|
| FindLaw Immigration Law | www.findlaw.com/01topics/20immigration/index.html |
| Hieros Gamos Immigration Law | www.hg.org/immig.html |
| Immigration Law Center on the Internet | www.legalsoft.net |
| Internet Law Library Immigration Law | law.house.gov/104.htm |
| LII Immigration and Naturalization Law Materials | www.law.cornell.edu/topics/immigration.html |
| LJX! Immigration Law | www.ljextra.com/practice/immigration/index.html |
| Siskind's Immigration Bulletin | www.visalaw.com/bulletin.html |
| USINS Immigration and Naturalization Laws | www.ins.usdoj.gov/law/index.html |
| **INTELLECTUAL PROPERTY** | |
| ABA Intellectual Property Section | www.abanet.org/intelprop/home.html |
| FindLaw Intellectual Property Law | $w^3$.findlaw.com/01topics/23intellectprop/index.html |
| FirstUse.com | www.firstuse.com |
| Hieros Gamos Intellectual Property Law | www.hg.org/intell.html |
| Intellectual Property Network | www.patents.ibm.com |
| Internet Law Library Intellectual Property Materials | law.house.gov/105.htm |
| IP Magazine | www.ipmag.com |

NOTE: Some browsers require http:// before the listed addresses  -  $w^3$ = www.

| | |
|---|---|
| LII Intellectual Property Materials | w³.law.cornell.edu/topics/topic2.html#intellectual property |
| LJX! Intellectual Property Center | w³.ljextra.com/practice/intellectualproperty/index.html |
| STO's Internet Patent Search System | metalab.unc.edu/patents/intropat.html |
| US Patent & Trademark Office | www.uspto.gov |
| USPTO Trademark Search System | www.uspto.gov/tmdb/index.html |
| USPTO Patent Search System | www.uspto.gov/patft/index.html |
| WWW Virtual Law Library Intellectual Law | www.law.indiana.edu/law/v-lib/intellect.html |
| **INTERNATIONAL** | |
| ABA International Law Section | www.abanet.org/intlaw/home.html |
| FindLaw International Law | w³.findlaw.com/01topics/24international/index.html |
| Hieros Gamos International Law | www.hg.org/internat.html |
| Internet Law Library International Materials | law.house.gov/89.htm |
| LII International Law Materials | www.law.cornell.edu/topics/international.html |
| LJX! International Law Materials | www.ljextra.com/practice/internat/index.html |
| Tufts U. - Multilateral Conventions Online | www.tufts.edu/fletcher/multilaterals.html |

NOTE: Some browsers require http:// before the listed addresses  -  w³ = www.

| | |
|---|---|
| WWW Virtual Law Library International Law | www.law.indiana.edu/law/v-lib/non-us.html |

**INTERNET**

| | |
|---|---|
| Computer Crime Directory | www.officer.com/c_crimes.htm |
| Cyberspace Bar Association | www.cyberbar.net |
| Electronic Privacy Information Center | www.epic.org |
| FindLaw Cyberspace Law Center | www.cybersquirrel.com/clc |
| Internet Library | www.phillipsnizer.com/internetlib.htm |
| J. Marshal Center for IT and Privacy Law | www.jmls.edu/cyber/index.html |
| LJX! Internet Law | www.ljx.com/internet |
| The Internet News Letter | www.ljx.com/newsletters/internet |
| The Legal Edge | web.jet.es/swift |
| The Cyberlaw Encyclopedia | gahtan.com/techlaw |

**LABOR & EMPLOYMENT**

| | |
|---|---|
| ABA Labor and Employment Law Section | www.abanet.org/labor/home.html |
| AFL-CIO | www.aflcio.org/home.htm |
| Department of Labor | www.dol.gov |

NOTE: Some browsers require http:// before the listed addresses - w³ = www.

| | |
|---|---|
| FindLaw Labor Law | www.findlaw.com/01topics/27labor/index.html |
| Hieros Gamos Labor Law | www.hg.org/employ.html |
| Internet Law Library Employment & Labor Law | law.house.gov/100.htm |
| LII Labor Law Materials | www.law.cornell.edu/topics/labor.html |
| LJX! Employment and Labor Law | w³.ljextra.com/practice/laboremployment/index.html |
| WWW Virtual Law Library Labor & Employ. Law | www.law.indiana.edu/law/v-lib/labor.html |
| **MARITIME/ADMIRALTY LAW** | |
| AdmiraltyLaw.com | www.admiraltylaw.com |
| International Maritime Organization | www.imo.org |
| LII Admiralty Materials | www.law.cornell.edu/topics/admiralty.html |
| Maritime Global Net | www.mglobal.com/ |
| NSNet | www.nsnet.com |
| Resources for Admiralty & Maritime Law | home.earthlink.net/~shiplaw/ |
| The Captain's Maritime Links | www.ime.net/~drwebb/maritime.html |
| **PROPERTY/REAL ESTATE** | |
| ABA Real Property, Probate and Trust Law Sec. | www.abanet.org/rppt/home.html |

NOTE: Some browsers require http:// before the listed addresses - w³ = www.

| | |
|---|---|
| FindLaw Property Law | www.findlaw.com/01topics/33property/index.html |
| Hieros Gamos Property Law | www.hg.org/realest.html |
| Internet Law Library Property Materials | law.house.gov/108.htm |
| LII Landlord/Tenant Materials | www.law.cornell.edu/topics/landlord_tenant.html |
| LII Real Estate Transactions Materials | www.law.cornell.edu/topics/real_estate.html |
| LJX! Landlord/Tenant Law Materials | www.ljextra.com/practice/landlordtenant/index.html |
| LJX! Real Estate Law Materials | www.ljextra.com/practice/realestate/index.html |
| Property Assessments Online | www.people.virginia.edu/~dev-pros/Realestate.html |
| WWW Virtual Law Library Property Law | www.law.indiana.edu/law/v-lib/property.html |
| **SECURITIES** | |
| FindLaw Securities Law | www.findlaw.com/01topics/34securities/index.html |
| FreeEDGAR | www.freeedgar.com |
| Global Securities Information, Inc. | www.gsionline.com |
| Hieros Gamos Securities Law | www.hg.org/security.html |
| Internet Law Library Securities Law | law.house.gov/320.htm |
| Legal Forms for Corp. and Securities Lawyers | www.jefren.com |

NOTE: Some browsers require http:// before the listed addresses - w³ = www.v

| | |
|---|---|
| SEC | www.sec.gov |
| SEC Edgar Database | www.sec.gov/edgarhp.htm |
| SECLaw.Com | www.seclaw.com |
| **TAX** | |
| ABA Tax Section | www.abanet.org/tax/home.html |
| FindLaw Tax Law | www.findlaw.com/01topics/35tax/index.html |
| Hieros Gamos Tax Law | www.hg.org/tax.html |
| Internet Law Library Tax Materials | law.house.gov/109.htm |
| IRS | www.irs.gov |
| LII Tax Materials | www.law.cornell.edu/topics/topic2.html#taxation |
| LJX! Tax Law Materials | www.ljextra.com/practice/taxation/index.html |
| TaxResources.com | www.taxresources.com |
| TaxWire | www.tax.org/TaxWire/taxwire.htm |
| The Tax Prophet | www.taxprophet.com |
| Uncle Fed.com | www.unclefed.com |
| WWW Virtual Law Library Tax Law | www.law.indiana.edu/law/v-lib/taxes.html |

NOTE: Some browsers require http:// before the listed addresses - w³ = www.

| TORT | |
|---|---|
| ABA Tort Section | www.abanet.org/tips/home.html |
| FindLaw Tort Law | www.findlaw.com/01topics/22tort/index.html |
| Hieros Gamos Tort Law | www.hg.org/torts.html |
| Internet Law Library Tort Materials | law.house.gov/110.htm |
| LII Tort Materials | www.law.cornell.edu/topics/torts.html |
| LJX! Tort Law Materials | www.ljextra.com/practice/negligence/index.html |
| OSHA | www.osha.gov |
| WWW Virtual Law Library Tort Law | www.law.indiana.edu/law/v-lib/tort.html |
| **WILLS, TRUSTS, ESTATES** | |
| FindLaw Probate, Trusts, & Estates | www.findlaw.com/01topics/31probate/index.html |
| Hieros Gamos Estate and Trust Law | www.hg.org/estate.html |
| Internet Law Library - Trusts & Estates | law.house.gov/112.htm |
| LII Estate & Gift Tax Materials | www.law.cornell.edu/topics/estate_gift_tax.html |
| LJX! Wills, Trusts, & Estates | www.ljextra.com/practice/trusts/index.html |
| Wills on the Web - Wills of Famous People | www.ca-probate.com/wills.htm |

NOTE: Some browsers require http:// before the listed addresses - w³ = www.

# GENERAL INTERNET RESEARCH

## MetaSearch Engines

[These engines search numerous other sites from one page]

| | |
|---|---|
| 800go | www.800go.com |
| Debriefing | www.debriefing.com |
| DogPile | www.dogpile.com |
| Highway61 | www.highway61.com |
| Mamma | www.mamma.com |
| MetaCrawler | www.metacrawler.com |
| Profusion | www.profusion.com |
| SavvySearch | www.savvysearch.com |

## Finding Places- Map Sites

| | |
|---|---|
| CyberAtlas | www.delorme.com/cybermaps |
| ETAK Guide | www.etakguide.com |
| MapQuest | www.mapquest.com |
| Maps On Us | www.mapsonus.com |
| YahooMaps | maps.yahoo.com/py/maps.py |

## General Search Sites

| | |
|---|---|
| Altavista | www.altavista.com |
| Ask Jeeves | www.askjeeves.com |
| Excite | www.excite.com |
| Google | www.google.com |
| GoTo.com | www.goto.com |
| Hotbot | www.hotbot.com |
| Infoseek | www.infoseek.com |
| LookSmart | www.looksmart.com |
| Lycos | www.lycos.com |
| Magellan | www.mckinley.com |
| Netscape | home.netscape.com |
| NewHoo! | www.newhoo.com |
| Northernlight | www.northernlight.com |
| Snap | www.snap.com |
| Web Crawler | webcrawler.com |
| Yahoo | www.yahoo.com |

NOTE: Some browsers require http:// before the listed addresses - w³ = www.

## Tracking/Mailing Packages

| UPS | www.ups.com | FEDEX | www.fedex.com/us |
|-----|-------------|-------|------------------|
| RPS | www.shiprps.com | USPS | www.usps.com |

## Finding Phone Numbers/Addresses

| | |
|---|---|
| 555-1212 Directory | www.555-1212.com |
| AnyWho | www.anywho.com |
| Excite People Finder | www.excite.com/reference/people_finder |
| Four11 Telephone Directory | www.four11.com |
| GTE Super Yellow Pages | www.superpages.gte.net |
| InfoSpace | infospace.com/index_ppl.htm |
| International Dialing Codes | www.the-acr.com/codes/cntrycd.htm |
| Internet 800 Directory | www.inter800.com |
| Switchboard | www.switchboard.com |
| U.S. Postal Service Zip Codes | www.usps.gov/ncsc |
| Yahoo Yellow Pages | yp.yahoo.com |
| Yahoo - People Search | people.yahoo.com |

NOTE: Some browsers require http:// before the listed addresses,

## Travel Related Sites

| | |
|---|---|
| Airline Phone Numbers & Web Sites | www.princeton.edu/Main/air800.html |
| Association of Business Travelers | www.abt-travel.com |
| Flifo Travel Agent | www.flifo.com |
| The Internet Travel Network | www.itn.net |
| TheTrip.com | www.thetrip.com |
| Travelocity Travel Agent | www.travelocity.com |
| Travelweb Agent | www.travelweb.com |

## News and Information

| | |
|---|---|
| ABC News | abcnews.go.com |
| Associated Press News Wire | wire.ap.org |
| C-SPAN | www.c-span.org |
| CBS News | www.cbs.com/navbar/news.html |
| CNN | www.cnn.com |
| LATimes | www.latimes.com |
| NBC News | nbc.com |
| News Edge Newspage | www.newspage.com |
| NY Times | www.nytimes.com |

NOTE: Some browsers require http:// before the listed addresses.

| USA Today | www.usatoday.com |
|---|---|
| WallStreet Journal | www.wsj.com |
| Washington Post | www.washingtonpost.com |

## Fee Based Information Gathering Tools

| KnowX | www.knowx.com | Public Records, Locate People, Research Businesses |
|---|---|---|
| The American Information Network Inc. | www.ameri.com | SHERLOCK - "[L]ocate missing persons, lost relatives or even track deadbeat spouses all using public records." I - D.M.V. - "[D]o a search of DMV records by Driver's License Number or a License Plate Number in 47 States for violations and registration information." |
| InfoTek Intelligent Information | www.cdb.com/public | "[T]ools to conduct searches for locating people and verifying business information and assets." |
| National Credit Information Network | www.wdia.com | Birth & Death Records, Credit Checks, Criminal History Checks, Voter Registration Info. SSN Tracing, Real Estate/ Property Records & More. |
| The Ultimates | www.theultimates.com | Search multiple resources like phone books, e-mail directories, and trip planners. Just type your search criteria into the first search engine and they are copied to others. |

# General Tips/Techniques

★ When searching for a company or entity try to use www.entityname.com
e.g. www.ford.com.

★ When a page does not load try to move "up" a level by deleting everything to the right of the
last "/" symbol in the URL address window. Keep trying this until the page will load.
e.g. www.legal.com/home/pages.htm will not load therefore try www.legal.com/home/ if this does not
load try www.legal.com/.

★ Use your browser's "find in page" or "find in frame" commands to locate words within text
intensive sites. In Nestscape Navigator 4.x & Internet Explorer 5.x go to Edit then select "Find in
Page".

★ Use your browser's "Open in New Window" command to utilize several browser windows at once. This
will GREATLY increase your researching speed. To use this feature simply place the cursor over the site
you would like to visit then click on the right mouse button and select "Open in New Window". Using this
command will NOT close the window from which you selected the next site but will minimize it instead. To
move between open/minimized windows click on the rectangular boxes located on the taskbar which lies
at the bottom of your screen.

# ADDITIONAL SITES

This guide was compiled by Shane A. Pollin. Mr. Pollin graduated from Tulane Law School with honors in 1998 and completed his undergraduate studies with honors from Vanderbilt University. While attending Tulane Law School he conducted extensive research into various Internet related legal topics including Internet telephony, maritime law resources on the Internet and family law resources on the Internet. Mr. Pollin has spoken publicly on the topic of Internet legal research and has been published in the *Tulane Maritime Law Journal*, an organization in which he held an editorial position.

If you are interested in utilizing Mr. Pollin's expertise on how to best use the growing number of legal resources in your practice please contact him at spollin@erols.com.